VIETNAM

A History From Beginning to End

Copyright © 2016 by Hourly History Limited

All rights reserved.

Table of Contents

Vietnam's Past
Exit the French
The United States and Ngo Dinh Diem
The Resistance War Against America Begins
"Americanization"
The American Home Front
Vietnamization and President Nixon
The End of the Vietnam War and Its Aftermath

Introduction

Although the country of Vietnam is a small corner of the globe, the Vietnam War was one of the most polarizing, iconic, and devastating events of the second half of the twentieth century. At its heart, the Vietnam War was a civil war fought between communist North Vietnam and South Vietnam; North Vietnam attempted to unite the two entities under a singular, communist government.

Although it was a civil war, because of the Cold War between the communist east and capitalist west, the role of communism in international policy, and the legacy of colonialism, the Vietnam War became a much broader conflict. In fact, when most people think about the Vietnam War, they probably think immediately of the involvement of the United States.

In reality, the Vietnam War is a truly transnational event, involving France, the United States, China, Cambodia, Laos, and the Soviet Union, as well as other nations.

For the United States, involvement in the Vietnam War divided its people, shook their faith in their own government, and sparked a protest movement that shifted the course of twentieth-century history. The most evocative images of 1960s America are those of hippies and anti-war protesters; in many ways, they define a generation.

However, the impact on the United States is nothing compared to the impact that the war had in Vietnam, as well as the neighboring countries of Cambodia and Laos, where the war raged. It was also a decades-long, devastating period of warfare and struggle for Vietnam, both North and South. It began as a war for independence, freedom from French colonialism and for self-rule, but it escalated into a conflict between east and west, and from which all combatants would find it impossible to extricate themselves.

Chapter One

Vietnam's Past

"If it were necessary to give the briefest possible definition of imperialism, we should have to say that imperialism is the monopoly stage of capitalism."

—Vladimir Lenin

Like so many places on the continent of Asia during the Age of Empire, the area that would become Vietnam was colonized by European powers. It was part of French Indochina, in the southeast corner of Asia. It shared a long border with China, and also contained present-day Laos and Cambodia.

Throughout the nineteenth century, the French became more and more involved in the region. Like many imperial ventures, they used the "white man's burden" as their reason, which was a thinly-masked racist justification for imperialism. Europeans and whites (including white Americans) believed that as a "superior race," they had a responsibility to "better" the "inferior races" of the world, such as Africans and Asians. Their mission often included spreading Christianity. The Vietnamese people (often referred to as the Siamese at the time), however, were not fooled by the rhetoric. Like others experiencing the same brand of colonization (the

Chinese included), they knew that these excuses were a thin guise used to justify the exploitation of their land, resources, and most tragically, their people.

As a result, the Vietnamese fought the encroachment of the French. A ten-year rebellion took place from 1885 to 1895. The Franco-Siamese War (a victory for the French) occurred in 1893 when the French sought to expand even further. By the dawn of the twentieth century, though, the French had largely consolidated their control in the region that would eventually contain Vietnam. Rebellions against the French continued in the region during the early twentieth century, but the French were almost always able to stop them quickly.

France maintained possession of Siam through the early decades of the twentieth century until World War II. World War II was truly a global war, but what most people do not realize is that it was not as simple as the Allied Powers fighting the Axis Powers. The fighting and the motivations for fighting were more complicated in several corners of the globe, and Indochina was one of them. Fighting broke out in Indochina against the French; the Siamese sought to take advantage of the fact that France was fighting a desperate war against Germany in Europe.

French Indochina faced bigger problems, though. In 1940, at the same time that they were attempting to overthrow the French, Japan invaded Indochina. Once France fell to Nazi Germany, the Vichy government that took over France was willing to negotiate with the Japanese.

It was around this time that the Viet Minh emerged. The Viet Minh, led by Ho Chi Minh, wanted independence: They did not want to be controlled by Japan any more than they wanted to be part of France. During this uncertain time of global warfare, Ho Chi Minh hoped to exercise agency over how world events would impact the outcome in their corner of the world.

The seeds of the Vietnam War were planted during the imperial struggles with France, and they germinated during World War II. At first, Ho Chi Minh and the Viet Minh attempted to hide their communist leanings and had the support of China (which had not yet become communist), which technically sided with the Allies in the war. World War II would last until 1945, but this struggle in Indochina was to last much, much longer.

Chapter Two

Exit the French

"Follow me if I advance! Kill me if I retreat! Revenge me if I die!"

—Ngo Dinh Diem

The years of World War II brought much suffering and destruction to nearly every corner of the globe, and Vietnam was no exception. The French accepted the presence of the Japanese in Vietnam in 1940. Japan occupied military outposts while the French auspices of government remained, though they, too, were largely controlled by the Japanese. This meant that fighting in Vietnam was not terribly severe; at the very least, the region saw relatively little conflict between the Allies and Axis because France was too preoccupied with fighting Germany at home to be concerned with fighting Japan in Vietnam.

However, other tragedies would strike Vietnam during this time. Vietnam was not a priority for either the French or the Japanese. The French were virtually absent, while the Japanese cared little for protecting the Indochinese people. So, when famine struck in 1944 (partially because of exploitation of resources on the part of the French and Japanese), little help was offered. As many as two million people perished. In addition to the impact of the loss of life, this large-scale suffering also polarized the opinions of the Vietnamese people regarding foreign governments.

Besides the terrible loss of life, the famine would have other far-reaching effects. Ho Chi Minh realized that hungry people are (rightfully) desperate and angry. Thus, he took advantage of the situation and raised a rebellion in which he urged the Vietnamese people to raid government supply warehouses and "steal" the food they so desperately needed. They were not unsuccessful; around one hundred warehouses were ransacked. What was more, the uprising raised the notoriety and the popularity of the Viet Minh and Ho Chi Minh as a national leader. Vietnamese people around the country lauded their efforts, and they won much support.

Then, in August 1945, the Japanese surrendered to the Allies, ending World War II. While much of the world welcomed peace, the period following this event was one of uncertainty for the Vietnamese. Japanese forces still occupied parts of their territory. They were technically no longer at war, so what was their role now? Also, how would Vietnam be governed moving forward? Would it be returned to France or granted independence? Might it be claimed by another Allied Power, especially the United States, since France had depended so heavily on other nations for victory?

The nationalist movement of the Viet Minh did not sit idly by while this transpired. In this period of uncertainty and transition, they fought for independence. Their August Revolution, which began around the beginning of the month, was initially very successful. Ho Chi Minh directed his followers to seize government buildings as well as military outposts and other critical sites. By the end of August 1945 (just over two weeks), the Viet Minh controlled almost every village and city—including very rural villages—in the country, including the capital of Hanoi. This led Ho Chi Minh to declare Vietnamese independence officially on September 2, 1945.

As might be expected, the western imperialist nations were not thrilled with events transpiring in Vietnam. However, they were understandably distracted by the end of World War II. Their neglect would not last long. In fact, foreign powers never actually left Vietnam. Chinese officials (who had been among the Allied forces), remained in what would become North Vietnam in order to help oversee the departure of the Japanese. As the Chinese entered the northern part of Vietnam, Ho Chi Minh lost political control, but certainly not his popularity. He remained an important leader, even though the Chinese were able to wrest control of Hanoi.

Meanwhile, south of the 16th parallel, Europeans were becoming more involved in Vietnamese affairs again, especially the French. The events of the First Indochina War are complex, and whole books have been written on it. Suffice it to say, for our purposes, that as France tried to re-take control of Vietnam, the Viet Minh, led by Ho Chi Minh, fought for independence throughout the following few years.

France remained poorly equipped to fight a war or even maintain control over a colony as they struggled to recover from the devastation of World War II at home. Finally, in 1949, France was forced to acknowledge the independence of Vietnam. However, this did not mean that they exited: they maintained much political and military presence in the new country.

Vietnamese independence was not the only major event in Asia in 1949. This was a momentous year, as it was also the year that China fell to communism, causing a global ripple effect in the Cold War going on between the United States and the Soviet Union.

Herein lays the origins of the Vietnam War and American involvement in Vietnam. The Cold War was guiding American foreign relations at the time. Chiefly, the United States believed in the Domino Theory and the policy of Containment, which followed it. According to the Domino Theory, communism needed to spread in order to survive, and communists would make every effort to cause this spread. As one country became communist, those nearby would thus be in danger of "falling" to communism as well. This "domino effect" would continue until communism had spread throughout the entire world, including the United States. Thus, it was imperative, in the minds of Americans and other westerners, that communism be "contained" where it was, which was the impetus for the policy of Containment. The United States would do just about whatever it took to prevent the spread of communism anywhere in the world, even in a small, seemingly insignificant corner of the globe like Vietnam.

In the minds of Americans, therefore, the waning power of the French was leaving a power vacuum in Vietnam, right next door to the newly communist China, who had already had a presence and been involved in Vietnamese affairs. At the same time, Ho Chi Minh and the Viet Minh were becoming more obviously, outwardly, communist in the policies they wished to enact.

Then, in 1950, American fears were realized when the Soviet Union and China recognized Ho Chi Minh's communist government in Vietnam, which had become very powerful in the north, with Hanoi as its seat of power. At the same time, the U.S., Great Britain, and other capitalist countries only recognized the French-controlled government in the southern part of the country, whose capital was located in the city of Saigon. Now, just as had happened in Korea (at the same time that the U.S. was becoming involved in fighting the Korean War to prevent the communist north from spreading communism to the south), a line was drawn between the communist north and capitalist south in Vietnam.

Fierce fighting continued over the next four years until finally, after the Battle of Dien Bien Phu, the French were forced to admit final defeat and exit Vietnam entirely. They met with Vietnamese leadership, as well as foreign leadership, in Geneva, Switzerland in 1954 for peace talks. The outcome of these talks was not immediate independence for Vietnam, which many Vietnamese people – Ho Chi Minh's followers especially – felt they had earned. The "Transition period" that followed would see growing involvement of the United States as France officially exited, as well as growing tensions between communists and anti-communists throughout the region.

Chapter Three

The United States and Ngo Dinh Diem

"We hold the truth that all men are created equal, that they are endowed by their Creator with certain unalienable rights, among them life, liberty and the pursuit of happiness."

—Ho Chi Minh, Independence Speech, September 2, 1945

The agreement of the Geneva Conference divided Vietnam at the 17th parallel. Elections were to be held, and the Vietnamese people were given three hundred days to move freely between north and south according to their cultural, social, or political beliefs. The United States launched a propaganda campaign in the north to entice people to settle in the south. The United States was now led by President Dwight Eisenhower, a former World War II commanding general who was also a Cold War hardliner in many ways, especially foreign policy. It was never a question for him and his administration whether the U.S. should be involved in Vietnamese affairs.

In the 1954 elections, Ngo Dinh Diem was put into power in South Vietnam. He was a popular figure in the U.S. and the west, a devout Catholic, and they supported his campaign. However, elections in neither the north nor the south were fair: despite proclamations of fairness, corruption was rampant on both sides, and this aura of corruption would hang over Diem throughout his years of power in Vietnam, which lasted until 1960.

Upon taking office, Diem began a campaign to consolidate control almost immediately. He had no intention of leaving office. Using the military, he launched brutal, repressive campaigns to eliminate all opposition. This is not to say that atrocities were not happening across the border, however. In North Vietnam, Ho Chi Minh also hunted his opposition and launched land reform programs that displaced many people and caused many other problems there. Vietnam—North and South—was suffering in its division.

Diem's repressive actions quickly engendered animosity among the people of South Vietnam, and an opposition movement emerged. Even though repression and other issues also prevailed in North Vietnam, more South Vietnamese began to think that perhaps backing Diem, or remaining in South Vietnam, had been a mistake. Whether communist or not, resistance against Diem's regime began to strengthen.

Diem met resistance with more repression, especially against any suspected communist activity. In 1955, he launched a program to seek out and persecute anyone suspected of communist activity. In less than three years, around 12,000 people were executed and 40,000 languished in prisons, many having been tortured or forced to endure very poor conditions.

Throughout all of this, Diem enjoyed the unwavering support of the United States and President Eisenhower. Since Diem opposed communism, America was on his side, at least for the time being. In fact, Diem visited the United States in 1957 and enjoyed a warm welcome, similar to that which any dignified head of state would have received. Because he was anti-communist and committed to stopping communism in his corner of the globe, none of his other behavior mattered as much to the Americans.

In some ways, Diem's repressive measures worked; communists and suspected communists were jailed and silenced. However, it also backfired; many more people within and outside of South Vietnam became aware of Diem's brutality and desired to either act against him or see others do so. Thus, between 1957 and 1960 a more organized and potentially more viable opposition movement arose domestically, calling itself the Vietcong (or Viet Cong). However, despite Diem's paranoid suspicions, it is not likely that the North Vietnamese played much of a role in dissension in South Vietnam at this point. Undoubtedly, Ho Chi Minh wanted to see the entire region united under one communist government (ideally led by himself), but North Vietnam was getting on its feet, so to speak, implementing their new government, reforms, and hunting dissidents within their own borders. Though they were keenly aware of and interested in what was happening to their southern counterparts, they were not yet interfering in South Vietnamese affairs.

Another cause of the resurgence of the Viet Cong (which was born from the Viet Minh, and also known as the National Liberation Front) was land reform. In North Vietnam, even though things were not perfect and very turbulent at first, land reform measures had been relatively successfully implemented. In South Vietnam, most of the population lived in rural villages, and they heard how their northern counterparts benefited from these reforms, which included redistribution. It was in their best interest to see them happen at home as well, and they thus began to consider at least the idea that nationwide communism might work for them. The conditions needed for a full-scale rebellion – a desire for specific changes among the majority of the population as well as political repression and persecution – were emerging in South Vietnam.

At the same time, even though they were not acting on their desires yet, North Vietnam was beginning to set its sights on expansion. Its leadership proposed expansion in the mid-1950s, but both the Soviet Union and China opposed it. North Vietnam would have depended on their support, and these leading communist nations felt that it was too risky at the time. Likely, the Korean War, involving the United States, played a role in their hesitation.

In the later years of the decade, however, they were ready. North Vietnam decided it would reinvigorate its attempts to expand communism to surrounding regions, especially in South Vietnam, but also possibly Laos and Cambodia. The first step was to get the Ho Chi Minh Trail functional again. The Trail was previously used to transport fighters as well as resupply them; it was a lifeline for the North Vietnamese, and they knew they would not be successful in South Vietnam without it. Its intricate nature and ability to conceal itself had allowed and would allow, North Vietnam to fight a guerrilla war, which would be disastrous for the United States.

The Trail was deliberately long and wound through dangerous terrain. This would make it difficult to locate, follow, or attack. It incorporated ancient paths used for trade and hunting, which meant that the help of local peoples and knowledge of the surrounding landscape was pivotal to its success. It also transcended national boundaries; North Vietnam deliberately went through Laos and Cambodia. They did this for two reasons: first, some of the leadership did not believe that these borders should be there. They identified culturally with the people living in these areas, and they shared a common past. Second, they knew that should the war involve foreign powers, attacking a technically non-combatant country would be problematic at best and blatantly illegal at worst for them. It was thus both a cultural and strategic decision.

By 1959, the North Vietnamese offensive was underway. They began by invading Laos, re-establishing the Ho Chi Minh Trail, and then invading the South from there. Within five years, around one hundred thousand North Vietnamese troops had infiltrated and were at war in South Vietnam. The United States would also be much more deeply involved by that time.

Chapter Four

The Resistance War Against America Begins

"I hate war as only a soldier who has lived it can, only as one who has seen its brutality, its futility, its stupidity."

—Dwight D. Eisenhower

In 1961, President Eisenhower's term was over, and President John F. Kennedy took the oath of office. Today, many associate the American Democratic Party with anti-war movements and Republicans with being more pro-war. However, during the Cold War, Democrats tended also to be quite hawkish. Kennedy was a "Cold Warrior," meaning that he very much believed in the Domino Theory and the policy of Containment. Even though he inherited American involvement in Vietnam, he escalated the situation.

Throughout the 1950s and early 1960s, Ngo Dinh Diem became increasingly unpopular. The United States recognized this and recognized that as he alienated more South Vietnamese people, they became more vulnerable to the appeals of North Vietnam and communism. Therefore, Kennedy and his advisers decided that Diem needed to be taken out of office. Before that, though, Kennedy tried other means to support South Vietnam.

American troops were initially sent to Vietnam under Eisenhower, who sent less than one thousand "military advisers" (this term would be used by the United States time and again in military interventions, including during the Iraq War in the 2000s). These numbers exploded during Kennedy's presidency; by the time that Kennedy was assassinated in November 1963, there were more than fifteen thousand troops American troops deployed in Vietnam.

In addition to aiding the South Vietnamese militarily, the U.S. also attempted to provide support in rural reform, recognizing that this was a major problem in the country. Even though the programs that the U.S. and South Vietnam implemented were meant to help the South Vietnamese people, they involved forcing people to relocate, which sometimes took people off of land that their families had inhabited for generations. Despite good intentions, these programs were fabulously unpopular and further engendered many South Vietnamese people against Diem and the United States, who were becoming more and more the same in their minds.

Eventually, Diem was overthrown. The events surrounding the coup against Diem were complicated. As the initial years of Kennedy's administration wore on, it became obvious that Diem did not have the ability to stop the North Vietnamese, which meant that he needed to be removed. Corruption within the South Vietnamese military was also a major factor.

While the United States and its Central Intelligence Agency (CIA) were involved in planning the coup, we do not yet have evidence that they completely orchestrated it (in the decades since the end of the Cold War in 1989, the United States has been declassifying documents related to foreign affairs that have changed the way historians understand many events, including the Vietnam War).

The CIA and President Kennedy and his advisers were well aware that a coup against Diem was planned. However, we have evidence that on November 2, 1963, after Diem was overthrown and executed, Kennedy himself was both shocked and troubled by Diem's death, which came just weeks before his own assassination.

Despite planning, South Vietnam did not become more stable without Diem. In fact, the opposite happened. Chaos assaulted the small country from outside and from within. From outside, North Vietnam took immediate advantage of the situation. They increased their troop presence and also began supporting South Vietnamese guerrilla fighters more openly and aggressively.

In the wake of the collapse of Diem's government, most of the people that tried to seize power in South Vietnam were military officials. This caused another problem for South Vietnam and the Americans: largely due to the long-term presence of American military advisers and some troops, the South Vietnamese people very much saw these military governments as "puppet regimes" of the United States, and that was very unpopular. What was more, North Vietnam was quick to exploit this suspicion with propaganda.

Historians have written entire books about the role of the United States during this period of transition and turmoil, asking what role the U.S. played in the eventual all-out war, what role the Cold War played, and what America should have done differently at this critical juncture to prevent the death and destruction that was to come. Suffice it to say that the biggest problems the United States had involved seeing events in Vietnam through a Cold War lens only, rather than interpreting the events and actions they the witnessed based on Vietnamese interests and beliefs. Americans only thought about the choice between communism, and not why the Vietnamese might be leaning in that direction. They also believed that military strength could defeat the North Vietnamese opposition and hold communism back. Within just a few years of Diem's execution and Kennedy's assassination, President Lyndon B. Johnson would lead a country embroiled in a foreign war that ripped apart public opinion at home.

Chapter Five

"Americanization"

"Our purpose in Vietnam is to prevent the success of aggression. It is no conquest, it is not empire, it is not foreign bases, it is not domination. It is, simply put, just to prevent the forceful conquest of South Vietnam by North Vietnam."

—President Lyndon B. Johnson

In popular memory, President Johnson is most closely associated with the Vietnam War. This is because, even though he did not start the war, his administration did escalate the war more than any other.

Johnson took the oath of office with lofty, liberal goals, especially after he was re-elected in a landslide in 1964. Chiefly, he wanted to solve the problems of civil rights that had plagued the country since before the Civil War. He also had an ambitious plan, called "the Great Society," to eradicate poverty in the United States. Whether his plans would have succeeded or not without the war can obviously not be known, but the war in Vietnam would distract Americans from and come to destroy most of his domestic agenda.

Johnson was not really in favor of the war in the first place. While he recognized the importance of containing communism globally, he was not as much of a "Cold Warrior" as Kennedy had been. Therefore, he wanted to end American involvement in Vietnam quickly. In fact, part of his 1964 election campaign platform involved achieving peace and not escalating the war in Vietnam.

Shortly before his re-election in November 1964, one of the major turning points of the war (at least concerning American involvement) occurred. In August, the North Vietnamese attacked a U.S. destroyer in the Gulf of Tonkin off the eastern shore of Vietnam. Johnson and his administration would claim that this attack was unprovoked, but the truth was that the United States was there helping South Vietnam attack North Vietnam.

This incident alone was not major, but what happened afterward changed the course of the war and Vietnamese history. In response, the United States Congress passed the Gulf of Tonkin Resolution. This resolution granted the president unprecedented war powers: more war powers than had been allowed during World War II.[1] Johnson and his advisers had a blank check and a free hand: they could do almost whatever they thought necessary, despite the financial costs, to win the war, with relatively little oversight from any other governing bodies. Johnson himself was quoted as commenting that the Resolution was "like Grandma's nightshirt, it covered

---

[1] Part of the ambiguity of this resolution revolved around the fact that the U.S. never actually declared war against North Vietnam. Therefore, constitutional laws that governed war powers did not apply, and Congress and the President could improvise, or at least work outside of these regulations.

everything." Since Johnson was so focused on his domestic agenda, he left the day-to-day handling of the war to his Secretary of Defense, Robert McNamara.

When most people think about the United States during the Vietnam War, they think about the protest movement (more about that below). In reality, most Americans supported their country's involvement in the war, at least initially. As a whole, Americans very much believed in the Domino Theory and believed that containing communism was absolutely critical. Therefore, when their country became more and more involved in the war in Vietnam to stop the spread of communism there, most of them did not question it - at least at first. Therefore, as the war escalated during the early years of Johnson's presidency, he believed that these actions reflected what Americans wanted, even though he was elected on the very opposite promise.

The war escalated quickly after Johnson's re-election. In April 1965, the U.S. initiated Operation Rolling Thunder. This transformed U.S. strategy: prior to this point, the U.S. military primarily reacted to North Vietnamese attacks; in other words, they fought on the defensive rather than offensive. When Rolling Thunder began, however, the U.S. began sustained attacks against the North Vietnamese and the Viet Cong. This involved large-scale air strikes and a massive influx of American troops.

As the war escalated throughout 1965, Johnson became desperate to end it. It was distracting from his Great Society reforms. He actually made peace overtures to the North Vietnamese in early 1965: if they surrendered, the United States would invest in social and industrial programs throughout Vietnam. However, for obvious reasons, the North Vietnamese rejected these peace offers. In response, Johnson became convinced that negotiations were pointless and took a harder line against the North Vietnamese. He ordered Secretary McNamara to be more aggressive.

Shortly thereafter, in June 1965, the CIA reported to Johnson and McNamara that Operation Rolling Thunder had had no effect since its implementation two months prior. Top U.S. generals advised them to send more troops. They complied, and this began the "Americanization" of the war. What this term meant was that the U.S. would not only act independently of the South Vietnamese military in the war, they would take the lead in the defensive against the North Vietnamese onslaught as well as launch more offenses against their strongholds. It was now as much an American war as it was a Vietnamese war, though many historians argue that it was long before this moment. At this point, though, the weakened South Vietnamese military and government took a backseat. They aided the Americans (especially in translating and communicating with villagers and guiding them through the country's terrain), but the war became America's fight.

The American troops were led by General William Westmoreland. Westmoreland espoused a strategy of attrition: he believed that if his forces were able to wear down the enemy and overwhelm them with constant attacks, they would be less able to respond and would weaken quickly. In other words, the Americans still believed that they could use their technologically superior military to defeat the Vietnamese fighting a guerrilla war.

Under this policy and led by Westmoreland, however, the war deteriorated rather quickly. Because the American forces were so focused on the war of attrition and weakening the enemy at all costs, the measure of success on their end became the body count: the more Viet Cong and North Vietnamese dead, the less able they were to wage war against South Vietnam effectively. "Shoot first" tactics undoubtedly cost many innocent lives, including civilians.

Another factor that very much worked against the Americans was the fact that they and their leaders were ill-equipped to fight a guerrilla war. Their most formative, modern military experiences had been in World War II, which was fought primarily on battlefields with large armies. Even in Korea, guerrilla warfare was not the primary means of fighting. However, in Vietnam, the North Vietnamese used small groups of fighters who knew the terrain and could slip in and out, and hide, more easily. They also made attempts to blend in and used sneak attacks and other similar tactics to not only inflict the maximum number of casualties that they were able to, but also to create an atmosphere of fear for their enemy. This is why there are relatively few major battles to speak of in the Vietnam War.

These tactics worked. As the war dragged on, American troops became more paranoid and demoralized. Since there were no real large battles, they could not rejoice in victory nor come together in defeat. They were often away from bases for long stretches at a time with only a few other men, contributing to their sense of isolation and disengagement. They were mostly young and were not equipped to deal with the hostility of the South Vietnamese people, whom they were supposed to be helping. They had not been taught to interpret this hostility as against the war itself, or a general suspicion of outsiders, especially westerners, in light of colonization. Instead, they often took it to mean that these people were sympathetic to the enemy, and possibly harboring Viet Cong fighters who might at any time attack.

This sense of fear was one of the biggest factors that caused atrocities to be committed throughout the course of the war. In what came to be known as "Zippo Raids," entire villages were burned to the ground. Whether because American troops were trying to cover up the fact that they had killed anyone in the village suspected of Viet Cong sympathies, or whether they wanted to prevent supplies from being passed to the enemy, Zippo Raids caused unimaginable hardship on the villagers who were displaced because of them.

Zippo Raids may have been effective in the short term, but they were also terribly short-sighted. The people who were displaced by them did not disappear; they were forced to seek refuge in nearby villages, where they naturally told of their hardships. South Vietnamese people who might have otherwise been more sympathetic to the Americans or at least neutral learned to hate

Americans and fear their arrival. This disconnect only led to more misunderstanding between the Americans and those they sought to protect, which led to more death and destruction.

As the war dragged on, the American public also became more skeptical and suspicious. Why wasn't it over? Why were more and more young people being sent to Vietnam, and why were so many of them getting killed? These questions came to preoccupy American media, and soon, the majority of the country had turned against the war.

Chapter Six

The American Home Front

"Don't you understand what I'm tryin' to say

Can't you feel the fears I'm feelin' today?

If the button is pushed, there's no runnin' away

There'll be no one to save with the world in a grave

Take a look around you boy, it's bound to scare you boy

And you tell me over and over and over again my friend

Ah, you don't believe we're on the eve of destruction"

—"Eve of Destruction," written by P.F. Sloan, performed by Barry McGuire

As discussed previously, most Americans generally supported the war when it began. For one thing, Americans believed that their own security was dependent on stopping the spread of communism everywhere in the world. For another, as we have seen, the war escalated gradually; no one knew that it would become a quagmire from which America would struggle to extricate itself, or that it would divide the nation so severely.

As the war waged on, President Johnson was plagued with anxiety that its failures (of which he was well-informed) would distract Congress from his domestic Great Society reforms. Therefore, he misled members of Congress about the progress of the war to distract them and push his own agenda.

However, he could no longer deny how badly things were going when in 1967, Secretary of Defense Robert McNamara, who had been in charge of the Vietnam War, resigned. What was more, he explicitly, publicly cited the futility of the war as the reason for resignation. Johnson was furious and frustrated at the same time: he was stuck with a war he never wanted that was now destroying his ambitious domestic reforms.

At this point, Congress realized that they had been misled, and wanted to re-take more control over the course of the war. However, it was not just Congress that lost faith in Johnson's credibility; the American people were becoming more informed about what was going on in Vietnam as well. The public became informed primarily through the press, as did many Congressmen. Especially in light of McNamara's resignation, the media started paying more attention to the realities in Vietnam. Evening television news started broadcasting footage from on the ground in Vietnam; for the first time, the realities of war were on display for all to see, and Americans were horrified. It was not so much that the war in Vietnam was necessarily more violent or destructive than past wars, but that so many people were watching it unfold. What was more, the media also began reading the names of the day's dead on the air, so Americans were keenly aware of the cost in American lives.

As this occurred, the American people realized that Johnson had been lying. The United States was not winning the war in Vietnam, nor were they even protecting the Vietnamese people. What came to be called the "credibility gap" developed: The American people perceived a gap between what Johnson said and what was really happening. And in the public mind, this did not only apply to Vietnam: since he had misled Congress and the American people about the war, they also had trouble trusting him on other issues. It is certainly true that the Vietnam War distracted from his Great Society initiatives, but it is also true that his own mishandling of the war cost him just as much.

Public opinion for the war worsened as it progressed because things were getting worse and worse. Perhaps more than any other event around this time, the Tet Offensive in January of 1968 revealed just how horribly the war was going for America and South Vietnam. On the night of the 30th, during the Tet holiday (Vietnamese New Year), the North Vietnamese and Viet Cong launched a surprise attack on American troops in several places simultaneously. Americans had no idea that the attack was imminent and were caught very much off-guard. Since the American news media had increased its presence in Vietnam, they were able to capture the entire event and televise the worst of it.

The Tet Offensive technically failed; in the end, it was a victory for the U.S. However, that mattered little.

American perception was that it should never have been able to happen in the first place if America was truly winning the war. It thus became a public relations nightmare for Johnson. His lies were revealed and confirmed in undeniable terms.

Less than three months later, another event occurred that crystallized American opinion about the war. On March 16, the My Lai Massacre took place. This event was essentially a Zippo Raid gone very, very badly wrong. As many as five hundred unarmed civilians in two small hamlets in South Vietnam were killed by U.S. troops, including men, women, children, and the elderly. Several of the women were also gang-raped, and bodies of many of the victims were mutilated.

Even though atrocities had been committed on both sides prior to the My Lai Massacre, this one was more dramatic for two reasons. First was the scale: the level of death and brutality was not by any means common during the war. Second, by this point, the press was well-positioned to make the American people aware of this kind of event. It also fit the narrative that had emerged from the war: it was an unmitigated disaster that was wreaking havoc on Vietnam rather than protecting it.

The troops who were involved in this terrible event eventually faced court martial. There had been attempts to cover up the Massacre, but they were relatively feeble, and the public saw through them. In the end, only one of the twenty-six men charged was convicted. Their common defense was that they acted on orders from their superiors. In all likelihood, the My Lai Massacre was probably the result of a combination of factors, not the least among them being an overwhelming sense of frustration and helplessness on the part of the troops that resulted in an explosion of pent-up rage.

Nevertheless, the event polarized public opinion in America. There was no in-between: Americans were either "hawks" or "doves," for the war or against it. Young people started taking to the streets in protest, burning draft cards,[2] and the Vietnam protest movement started to gain momentum.

After McNamara's resignation, Clark Clifford became the new Secretary of Defence. Shortly following the My Lai Massacre, he reported to Johnson that there had been no measurable progress in Vietnam for *four years*—more than Johnson's entire presidency. What was more, his worst fears were realized: he had largely been unable to enact his Great Society reforms. While some of them were enacted, public attention was d^{2}istracted by the war, and even those that were put into law were largely ignored by the public. Johnson knew his administration was ruined and that the war was a lost cause. In light of these failures, he announced that he would not run for re-election in 1968.

---

[2] The use of the draft in the Vietnam War would be a major issue, and one that came to symbolize the protest movement. However, it is worth noting that the draft was not being used at this point; young men had to register for the draft as they had been required for many years, but no one was actually being drafted to fight in the war at this point. The draft would not be used until President Nixon was in office.

At the same time, the protest movement against the war was an undeniable force in American politics and culture. The protest movement was part of what has come to be called the "New Left" in this era of United States history. It was only since the administration of Franklin D. Roosevelt in the 1930s and 1940s that the Democratic party had been associated with liberalism in America. However, President Johnson was a Democrat also, and as the lies and failures of Vietnam were revealed, many left-leaning Americans came to see him as just as bad as more conservative Republicans, at least when it came to the war.

Not only that but other simultaneous movements were at hand as well, which combined to create an atmosphere of upheaval in the United States. By the late 1960s, the United States had been embroiled in the Civil Rights Movement for almost two decades. This was a struggle to extend equal rights promised by the Constitution to African American citizens, especially in the racist, segregated southern states. By the late 1960s, violent retribution was still being visited upon those who joined this fight, and people were frustrated. What was more, in April 1968 the Reverend Dr. Martin Luther King, Jr. was assassinated. King had come to symbolize the movement as its figurehead; he had led a bus boycott in 1954 that had helped catalyze the movement and had largely directed it since then.

At the same time, there was also a burgeoning women's rights movement of women who wished to fight against sexism and discrimination that relegated their worth only to their roles as wives and mothers, subservient to men. The combination of these movements led liberal "radicals" to feel unhappy and frustrated with the status quo; they were enraged with the war and white supremacist terrorism that continued to plague the nation. Their anger came to focus so much on the war because they believed that it distracted lawmakers and the public from America's real issues at home: extending equal rights to all peoples, regardless of skin color, gender, or other factors.

The counter-culture or the "hippie" movement of the mid-late 1960s has come to symbolize not only the protest movement and the "New Left" but also the entire era in popular memory. However, this youth revolt was actually rather small. It is important to note that while many Americans turned against the war and did not support it, only a tiny fraction of the U.S. population actively took part in the counter-culture "hippie" movement. It is only because they received huge media attention that they loom so large in our collective memory.

Their anger was the result of not only resistance to civil rights, not only the pointless war but also Cold War conformity and consumerism. This is why they openly rejected social norms in the way that they dressed, behaved, and lived. They believed that normal politics and mainstream ways of life had failed to enlighten society and extend human rights, so they sought extra-political activities. They began by participating in protest rallies and marches, but they got stranger than that. They held what came to be called "Be-Ins," a play on the sit-ins that had been a popular means of protest in the Civil Rights movement. During a "Be-In," hippies occupied public space, and would often do "abnormal" things in order to attract attention to themselves, like playing music or performing street theater.

Other major aspects of the hippie movement were open drug use and promiscuous sex. These were two of the major ways in which they flaunted social norms. The Cold War "culture of conformity" had made this sort of behavior taboo, which was one reason that they engaged in it. However, in a more genuine way, they also sincerely believed that these activities would help them "free their minds" and discover more about themselves and their fellow human beings.

The hippie movement, as liberal as it was, was not completely disorganized. The summer of 1967 came to be called the "Summer of Love," in which one hundred thousand hippies converged on the city of San Francisco, California. This event more than any other attracted massive media attention and public fascination, as it was an unprecedented gathering of youths. True to their culture, they openly used drugs, embraced "free love," and lived communally.

Then, in the summer of 1969, the event that perhaps best symbolized the hippie movement occurred: Woodstock. Located actually nearly fifty miles from the upstate New York town of Woodstock, this was three-day music festival took place on a dairy farm in Bethel Woods, roughly one hundred miles north of New York City. Music was a huge part of the counter-culture, and some of the biggest performers of the day were on the stage at

Woodstock, including Janis Joplin, Jimi Hendrix, Joan Baez, The Grateful Dead, Joe Cocker, and The Who. Regardless of its association with the counter-culture, the Woodstock Music Festival remains one of the most important events in modern music history.

A lot of things went wrong at Woodstock. First, far more people converged on this small town than anticipated, which caused other problems, including a shortage of food, water, and bathrooms. The weather was also bad: it rained, and the farm fields where the festival was held became very muddy. However, despite these real, serious issues, the event unfolded with almost no violence or other problems. The world watched as these hippies lived up to their principles of love, peace, and kindness.

Who were the hippies? While we tend to remember them as radicals, in reality, they had more "normal" origins. They were mostly young, white, and from middle-class families. Many of them were college students, which is part of the reason why some of their most important events took place in the summer—school was not in session. As the years wore on, many of them "retired" to more mainstream lives, with jobs and families.

Nonetheless, the hippie movement had a lasting impact on American liberalism, as well as American conservatism (a significant conservative backlash crystallized in the 1970s). They also had a lasting impact on American popular culture, not only by their memory but also because much of what they did eventually went mainstream. While their styles of communal living and free love were not widely embraced, they did provide free medical clinics and established job co-ops, practices that have spread since then. In addition, cultural and material phenomena promoted by the hippies have also become mainstream in the United States, like organic foods and whole grain bread. Also, a few hippie businesses went mainstream, including Celestial Seasonings Tea and *Rolling Stone Magazine.*

Nonetheless, the hippie movement was divisive in the years of the 1960s as the war still raged. They were an extreme example of a popular sentiment on the war. By the late 1960s, most Americans wanted out of the war. In 1968, Republican Richard Nixon was elected president, representing a desire for a change in American foreign policy. While he promised to end the war, things would get much worse before they got better.

Chapter Seven

Vietnamization and President Nixon

"No event in American history is more misunderstood than the Vietnam War. It was misreported then, and it is misremembered now."

—Richard M. Nixon

Many Americans expected Richard Nixon to be a Cold War hard-liner. However, he surprised critics and members of his own party by issuing the "Nixon Doctrine" early in his term. The Nixon Doctrine, which guided Nixon's foreign policy, wanted to reduce the importance of the Cold War against the USSR in American foreign relations. He wanted to broaden U.S. foreign policy, and not make concerns about the Soviet Union so important (he also wanted to reduce the power of the USSR).

However, the Nixon Doctrine would not alleviate conditions in Vietnam. When it came it Vietnam, Nixon ran for President promising peace, but in reality, he would actually escalate the war. Contrary to his Nixon Doctrine, he was still determined not to "lose" South Vietnam to communism.

In 1969 (the year Nixon took office), Ho Chi Minh, the North Vietnamese leader, died. Nixon saw this as an opportunity to shift the burden of the war back onto the South Vietnamese people, since he supposed that North Vietnam would be chaotic, trying to re-consolidate power without their dictator. As opposed to "Americanization" of the war, therefore, he initiated "Vietnamization." In addition to relying more on the South Vietnamese militarily, Nixon wanted to shift the focus of American efforts to more bombing and fewer troops in combat (that would be South Vietnam's new role).

Nixon and his advisers, including Secretary of State Henry Kissinger, wanted this bombing to be strategic: to hit fewer civilian targets and inflict more damage on the North Vietnamese ability to wage war. As discussed earlier, they knew that the Viet Cong used supply lines that ran through other countries, especially Laos and Cambodia. Therefore, in order to stop them, Nixon ordered secret, illegal bombing of Vietcong supply lines in Cambodia especially.

The result of these decisions was absolutely disastrous for both Cambodia and Laos. In Cambodia, a civil war broke out that eventually killed one million people. In Laos, land mines placed by the United States are still exploding, killing and maiming innocent people up to the date of this writing.

In addition, while these actions were supposed to be secret, eventually, the world found out. It reinvigorated the anti-war movement. Renewed energy and outrage sparked more protests and demonstrations. College campuses erupted in violence as police sometimes responded brutally to protestors. At Kent State University in Ohio, four students were killed in a demonstration, and two were killed in a protest at Jackson State University in Mississippi.

The war was certainly in a state of transition during Nixon's early years as President. Although he had promised to end the war, it escalated and spread to neighboring countries. This prompted the U.S. government to restrict the President's role in fighting the war. In response to the violence, and especially in response to the horrific illegal activities in Cambodia and Laos, Congress revoked the Gulf of Tonkin Resolution, which had given President Johnson (and then President Nixon) unprecedented war powers. They realized that giving the president that degree of power—regardless of who held that office—was dangerous.

Another major turning point in the Vietnam War was also about to occur: use of the draft. Many associate the draft with a much earlier point in the war, because young men had burned their draft cards before this point in protest of the war, but it was not actually used until December of 1969, and the protest surrounding the draft did not reach its apex until it was actually used. The draft was drawn by lottery based on the draftees' birthday. Young men were drafted for one-year tours in Vietnam.

The use of the draft at this time coincided with other movements, especially the Civil Rights Movement, and the anger that inspired protest in both was in some ways compatible. Young men whose birthdays were drawn in the draft could receive an exemption, or deferment, under specific circumstances. This included medical excuses and attendance in college. For obvious reasons, wealthy, white men were more likely to be in college than less advantaged black men. But even medical exemptions were easier for privileged people to get because of access to better lifelong healthcare. African American men had already served disproportionately in Vietnam. At the same time, they faced violence and prejudice at home. Many of them did not wish to serve since they did not feel the war was beneficial to them or to the Vietnamese people either. The draft not only caused protests around the country, but also cultivated deep class resentment between the poor, who could not get a deferment, and middle and upper-class people who could.

The implementation of the draft was followed in April-July of 1970 by major ground operations in Cambodia by U.S. troops, both to combat the growing domestic unrest in that country and attempt to push back the Vietcong and their supply lines. Nixon promised to end the war, but like Johnson, he found himself more and more embroiled in it, unable to extricate his country from the conflict. During his first term the war had escalated and even spread to neighboring countries; Vietnamization was failing.

In March 1972, just a few months before Nixon was to face re-election in the coming November elections, North Vietnam began a massive, unprecedented attack on South Vietnam. This was more than the guerrilla tactics they had relied on before; now, the might of the North

Vietnamese army (aided by other communist regimes) bore down on South Vietnam.

President Nixon felt he had no choice but to respond. Even at this point in the war, he still felt he could not let South Vietnam fall to communism. What was more, the South Vietnamese would not consent to withdrawal on the part of the United States. They openly admitted that they would likely be forced to surrender if the U.S. backed out and desperately needed continued U.S. support.

Oddly enough given the situation in Vietnam at the time, the Cold War and even the Vietnam War helped President Nixon win re-election. Despite escalating tensions in Vietnam, he had softened relations with China and even with the Soviet Union. What was more, his Democratic opponent, Senator George McGovern, vowed to exit Vietnam immediately, and Nixon used this and some of his other policies to paint McGovern as a dangerous radical.

Thus the Vietnam War survived another presidential election, and U.S. involvement stretched into the mid-1970s. Despite overwhelming public opinion against the war, despite continued promises to exit, and even despite politicians' hatred for the war, American troops remained on the ground in Vietnam. The reasons are complex, and most have been explored already, though certainly the Cold War policy of containment and dedication to preventing Vietnam from "falling" to communism played huge roles in America's decision making.

Chapter Eight

The End of the Vietnam War and Its Aftermath

"I saw courage both in the Vietnam War and in the struggle to stop it. I learned that patriotism includes protest, not just military service."

—John F. Kerry

How did the Vietnam War end (at least for the United States)? It ended much as it began: ambiguously. In December 1972, the U.S. initiated massive bombing raids against North Vietnam. This was largely in retaliation for the invasion launched by the North Vietnamese against South Vietnam in March.

By all accounts, the bombing raids were successful, but at a high cost. Many civilians were killed, and important infrastructure was destroyed. Nonetheless, by January 1973, the North Vietnamese were willing to negotiate, and they sat down with the South Vietnamese to peace talks.

At this point, after his re-election was secure, President Nixon decided to withdraw American involvement in Vietnam. Since the United States had never formally declared war, they did not need to be part of the negotiations or sign a peace treaty with either side.

He declared victory because North Vietnam had asked for peace negotiations, and began troop withdrawal.

Even though peace negotiations commenced, and even though both sides had agreed to negotiate, the U.S. withdrawal—as appropriate and necessary as it was for the United States—spelled disaster for South Vietnam. Two years later, in the spring of 1975, Saigon—the capital of South Vietnam—fell to the North Vietnamese. Americans were still stationed in offices and outposts in the city as they dismantled the war apparatus and worked to help South Vietnam transition. When the city fell, however, the last remaining military officials and diplomats were forced to flee and flee quickly. They packed into helicopters as desperate South Vietnamese citizens clamored to climb aboard, and these dramatic images of desperation became the symbol of the end of the Vietnam War, which was thus represented much as it had been all along: with chaos, suffering, and disorganization.

The fall of Saigon was especially poignant in light of the costs of the war. More than 58,000 Americans lost their lives fighting the war. More dramatically, more than one million Vietnamese people died, in addition to another million deaths in Cambodia, most a result of the civil war that broke out after the U.S. commenced secret bombing.

The war also combined with other events, such as the slow-moving Civil Rights Movement in the United States, to shatter a perceived sense of innocence in the U.S. Whether this actually ever existed is up for debate, but certainly, the sentiment in the U.S. had shifted. People lost faith in their leaders and no longer trusted the government. It would be years before trust was restored (especially after Nixon's scandals and illegal activities forced him to resign), and in some ways, it never was.

One of the most devastating effects of the Vietnam War in the United States was the treatment of veterans and the role that post-traumatic stress disorder would play in their lives. Quite unfortunately, war protesters sometimes focused their anger on soldiers returning from war. They blamed them for the atrocities that were being committed in Vietnam. Coupled with the horrific, traumatizing experiences of fighting in the war, this anger directed toward them upon return would have devastating effects on the rest of their lives. Vietnam veterans suffered from alcoholism, addiction, depression, violent tendencies, suicide, and other issues in higher proportions than other wars.

In addition, prisoners of war remained a major issue for the United States. The newly formed Socialist Republic of Vietnam was slow to release American POW's. Many of them were tortured before being returned. The American government would continue to search and advocate for missing men, though many believe that they did not do enough. To this day, there is still a long list of men who never returned from the fighting in Vietnam.

Thus, the war continued to inflict tragedy and suffering in the United States. It did the same in Vietnam. Soon after reuniting, Vietnam became embroiled in the brutal war across the border in Cambodia, and more of their people died. Their relationship with China also deteriorated, because China saw Vietnamese involvement in Cambodia as a threat to their control over the region. Vietnam's economy continued to suffer, partially because it maintained a massive military. After the Cold War had ended, however, it scaled back its military and began a slow transition to capitalism.

Conclusion

The Vietnam War remains one of the most poignant events of the Cold War for the United States. It polarized public opinion and revealed the problems with the Domino Theory and the policy of containment. Though the Korean War had been relatively successful for the U.S., Vietnam showed that these policies were not only unsustainable but also immensely, immeasurably destructive.

The Vietnam War also came to symbolize an era of American history. When Americans remember the 1960s, they think of America's involvement in Vietnam. They visualize the hippies and the protest movement. When they talk about President Kennedy, or President Johnson, or President Nixon, their Vietnam policies are usually some of the first issues that come to mind.

The Vietnam War also symbolizes the end of an era, in several ways. First, the protest movement that it inspired helped to end the early Cold War culture of conformity. The events of Vietnam, coupled with the violence of the Civil Rights Movement, also shook America's confidence in its ability to solve its own as well as the world's problems. It revealed inherent hypocrisies in American domestic and foreign policies, undermining the policy of containment that had guided foreign policy for more than twenty years. In short, it represented an end of innocence.

Of course, all of this pales in comparison to the impact that the war had on its own people, in Vietnam. The small country struggled for decades to rebuild from the destruction and devastation of the war, not to mention the impact of the tremendous loss of life and injury. It has only been in recent years that Vietnam has strengthened its economy and showed signs of permanent recovery.

Because of its vast real and symbolic importance, Vietnam has frequently been portrayed in American culture as well. In addition to the countless protest songs that were produced during the war, there have also been films made about it across a broad range of genres. Masterpieces like *Platoon* and *Apocalypse Now* reveal the brutal nature of the war, and the toll it took on individuals.

The war has also been memorialized worldwide. The American Vietnam Veterans Memorial on the National Mall in Washington, D.C. is an iconic symbol of America during the war. It is a long, black wall with the names of the Americans killed in action engraved upon it. It stretches over two acres. It is reflective so that those who look upon it see themselves behind the names. Its darkness symbolizes how dark and divisive this period in American history was, and the names remind visitors of the real human toll of war. A valid criticism of this memorial, however, is the fact that it does not acknowledge the impact of the war on Vietnam. Other memorials, though, exist in other places throughout the world, including more than two dozen in Vietnam.

In the end, many who still remember the Vietnam War in America wonder why the United States fought in the first place. For the Vietnamese people, this question matters as well. More important is the impact that the war had on their land, their people, and the way they still envision themselves as a nation.

Printed in Great Britain
by Amazon